# Body Sculpting

Sally Morgan

Heinemann
LIBRARY
Chicago, Illinois

© 2006 Heinemann Library
a division of Reed Elsevier Inc.
Chicago, Illinois

Customer Service 888-454-2279

Visit our website at www.heinemannlibrary.com

Illustrations by Nick Hawken
Originated by Repro Multi Warna
Printed and bound in China by SCPC Company Limited

10 09 08 07 06
10 9 8 7 6 5 4 3 2 1

**Library of Congress Cataloging-in-Publication Data**
Morgan, Sally.
  Body sculpting / Sally Morgan.-- 1st ed.
    p. cm. -- (Science at the edge)
  ISBN 1-4034-7762-0 (library binding - hardcover)
  1. Surgery, Plastic--Juvenile literature. I. Title. II. Series.
  RD119.M655 2005
  617.9'5--dc22
                                    2005024169

**Acknowledgements**
The Publishers would like to thank the following for permission to reproduce photographs: American Society of Plastic Surgeons p**24**; Alamy Images/Lou Linwei p**57**; Corbis (Gregory Pace) p**45**, (Jeffrey L Rotman) p**28**, (Jose Luis Pelaez Inc) p**39**, (Kevin R Morris) p**6**; Corbis Saba/Najlah Feanny p**22**; Corbis Sygma pp**31**, **50**, (Bob Collier Photos) p**20**, (Patrick Robert)p**37**; Empics/Associated Press p**5**; Getty Images (Stone) p**8**; Getty Images/Imagesource p**47**; Harcourt Education Ltd (Nick Hawken) p**26**; Mediscan p**19**; PA Photos p**9**; Reuters (Gary Hershorn) p**40**; Science Photo Library p**51**, (W Industries/James King-Holmes) p**54**, (BSIP, LA/Caby Valence) p**48**, (Coneyl Jay) pp**32**, **36**, (Custom Medical Stock Photo) p**33**, (Custom Medical Stock Photo/M Marshall) p**43**, (Custom Medical Stock Photo/Michael English) p**11**, (Dr P Marazzi) p**18**, (John MacFarland) p**10**, (Lauren Shear) p**34**, (Mauro Fermariello) p**13**, (Michelle Del Guercio) pp**14**, **42**, (MIT AI Lab/Surgical Planning Lab/Brigham & Women's Hospital) p**53**, (Pascal Goetgheluck) pp**15**, **29**; Wellcome Trust pp**17**, **46**.

Cover photograph of cosmetic eyelid surgery reproduced with permission of Science Photo Library (Coneyl Jay).

The Publishers would like to thank Mr. V. Ilankovan, Consultant Maxillofacial Surgeon, for his assistance in the preparation of this book.

Every effort has been made to contact copyright holders of any material reproduced in this book. Any omissions will be rectified in subsequent printings if notice is given to the Publishers.

# Contents

# Introduction

In 1992 Louise Ashby was 22 years old and dreamed of an acting career in Hollywood. One night, as she and a friend were driving home, another car crashed into theirs. Louise was seriously injured, and the left side of her face was nearly destroyed.

A few decades earlier, Louise would have had to learn to live with her disfigured face. But over a period of ten years, her appearance was gradually restored to normal thanks to advances in the field of plastic surgery.

## Plastic surgery

The word *plastic* in plastic surgery does not refer to plastic materials. Another meaning of the word plastic is "capable of being molded or of receiving form," and this is what is meant by the term plastic surgery. Plastic surgery involves processes such as moving skin and tissue from one part of the body to another and reshaping other parts of the body.

There are two uses for plastic surgery—reconstructive surgery and cosmetic surgery. Reconstructive surgery is carried out in order to restore a more normal appearance to abnormal or injured parts of the body, as in the case of Louise Ashby. Common procedures in reconstructive surgery are repairing wounds and repairing fractures of the facial bones. Other examples include removing skin cancers, repairing genetic defects, and repairing skin damage caused by burns.

Cosmetic surgery is performed to improve the appearance rather than to correct injuries or abnormalities. Common kinds of cosmetic surgery include facelifts, nose reshaping, and fat removal. In recent years there has been an increase in the popularity of cosmetic surgery in richer countries, particularly in the United States. In 2002 nearly 7 million cosmetic procedures (both surgical and non-surgical) were performed in this country—more than three times the number in 1997. More than 80 percent of those who had cosmetic surgery were women, although the number of men having plastic surgery has risen rapidly in recent years.

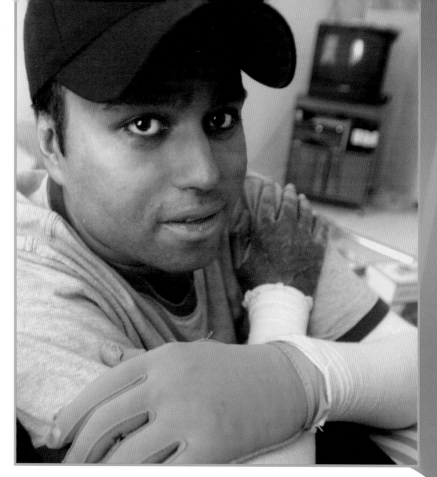

On September 11, 2001, Manu Dhingra arrived for work at the World Trade Center just as the first plane hit. He made it down 83 flights of stairs to safety, but he suffered severe burns on his face, arms, stomach, and back. He had to undergo several painful operations to repair the damage. After his release from the hospital, he said he was grateful for this second chance at life.

## Cosmetic concerns

Plastic surgery raises many issues. As advances in technology mean that more procedures can be carried out more easily, there are increasingly difficult questions to consider. What happens when cosmetic surgery goes wrong? Should young people have cosmetic surgery? Is it ethical for doctors to completely change the appearance of their patient? In this book you can read about plastic surgery and learn more about these issues. You can learn about the techniques used by surgeons and the science behind the technology. Also find out how technologies such as cloning, brain transplants, and virtual reality may shape the future of plastic surgery. Decide for yourself whether cosmetic surgery is a good or bad thing.

# The Rise of Plastic Surgery

Reconstructive surgery was probably first used in India in approximately 600 B.C.E., when doctors used skin from the forehead to rebuild the noses of people who had had them cut off as punishment. However, it was not until the development of anesthesia, toward the end of the 19th century, that the first real advances in plastic surgery took place.

There were further major developments during World War I. Thousands of soldiers were badly wounded on the battlefield. Never before had such large numbers of soldiers been so severely injured. Doctors, such as the French army surgeon Hippolyte Morestin, had to learn how to deal with severe facial injuries, burns, and lost limbs. It was from these first experiences of reconstructive surgery that surgeons developed techniques for plastic surgery on the nose and the face. Advances in reconstructive surgery were also made during World War II.

During the 1950s implants to enlarge breasts were used for the first time, and liposuction (the removal of fat) was developed in the 1970s. Since then plastic surgery has developed rapidly, mainly because of advances in equipment—for example, the development of endoscopes and laser surgery.

## What is beautiful?

Many people have cosmetic surgery in order to make themselves more beautiful. But what is considered unattractive in one society can be considered beautiful in another, and vice versa. sociological

In some cultures, heavier weight is seen as an indication that a person is healthy and well off. In many parts of West Africa, for example, a full body is considered highly desirable and linked to fertility. In some cultures young women planning to get married eat heavily before their wedding in order to put on as much weight as possible. In fact, there is medical evidence to suggest that women who have fat around their hips and less on their waist are less likely to suffer from infertility problems.

In Western society, slimness is considered attractive. Some people even undergo cosmetic surgery to remove fat.

> *"Until I came to America, I never knew thin was beautiful."*
>> Young male exchange student from the Ivory Coast

In many cultures, exaggerated features such as extra-large ear lobes, big lips, long necks, or tiny feet are considered attractive. For instance, some Senegalese women increase the natural thickness of their upper lip by pricking it repeatedly until it is permanently inflamed and swollen. Does this sound similar to the way certain celebrities in the United States make their lips bigger with chemicals or surgery?

In the Karen Padaung tribe of Burma, a long neck is considered beautiful. When a girl reaches the age of five, she is given her first neck ring, and as she gets older, new ones are added. The rings stretch her neck until it is about 12 inches long. In some areas the Karen Padaung put large pieces of ivory in their ear lobes instead of wearing neck rings.

## Lotus feet

One of the more extreme examples of altering parts of the body is the ancient Chinese custom of foot binding. Tiny feet, called lotus feet, were considered a sign of beauty and attractiveness in women. Young girls from wealthy families would have their feet bound when they were about five years old. Their toes were bent under, and bones were broken to force the front and back of the foot together. At the end of this binding process, the young girls had feet about four inches long! However, these tiny feet meant that the girl could not walk properly and often had to be carried.

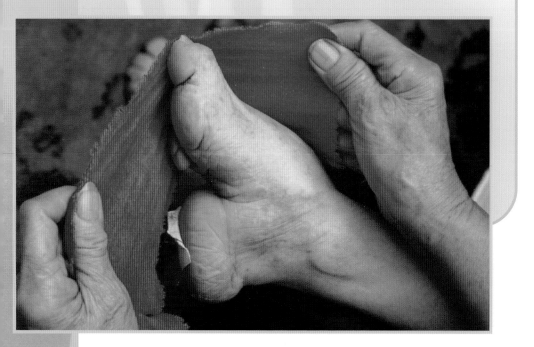

## Media pressure   *sociological*

Today there is pressure from many sources to be young and slim. Apparently perfect faces and bodies appear on magazine covers and TV screens and stare down from billboards. It is not surprising that young people today worry about their appearance, and that many older men and women try to look younger.

However, what you see in photos and on films can be an illusion. Faces are often retouched to remove the slightest spot, blemish, or wrinkle. Sometimes photos are stretched to make a person look taller and thinner. In films, actors often have a body double—someone with a fit, muscular body who stands in for the actor in some shots.

In an attempt to live up to these ideals, more people than ever are undergoing plastic surgery, especially cosmetic surgery. In the past more women have had cosmetic surgery, but the number of men having cosmetic procedures is growing fast. They now make up about twenty percent of plastic surgery patients, double the percentage of fifteen years ago.

## Risky business

All surgery is risky, and plastic surgery is no different. Reconstructive procedures can be long and complex, and things can go wrong. Doctors warn patients about the risks, but for many people, the benefits of a normal appearance far outweigh any risk.

Cosmetic surgery is different. Patients choose to have surgery in order to change their appearance. So is the risk worth it? Not surprisingly, patients are very unhappy when things go wrong and they end up with a disfigured face or a scarred body. They may need to have further operations to correct the mistakes of the first one.

The singer and actress Cher makes no secret of the fact that she has had cosmetic surgery.

The problems caused by mistakes in plastic surgery are not just physical. Patients can suffer emotionally and psychologically as well. Often the victims of mistakes feel guilty or think that they are being punished for vanity. As cosmetic surgery increases in popularity, it becomes more and more important to be aware of the risks.

# The Plastic Surgeon's Toolbox

In recent decades new procedures have transformed plastic surgery. Today's surgeons can suck fat out of the body, move tissues from one area to another, and rebuild damaged parts using bone and muscle from another area. In order to carry out these complex operations, surgeons need specialist equipment and techniques. This chapter takes a closer look at the plastic surgeon's toolbox.

## Endoscopy

The endoscope is an instrument that allows a surgeon to look inside the body without opening it up. It consists of a snake-like tube containing optical fibers connected to a tiny camera and a bright light. The tube is inserted through a small incision (cut) and positioned until the end reaches the site where the surgeon wants to operate. The optical fibers send images from the surgical site to a tiny camera. The images are magnified on a viewing screen, allowing the surgeon to view the surgical site almost as clearly as if the body had been cut open.

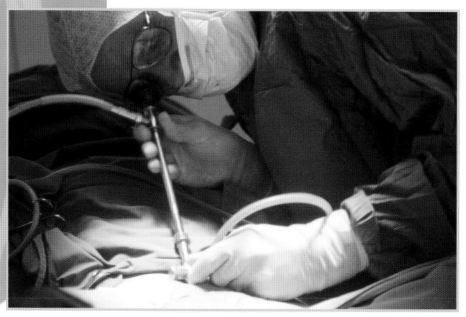

During an endoscopic operation, the surgeon views the operation using a video camera attached to a tube containing optical fibers. The tube is inserted into the body. Surgical instruments are inserted through one or more other tubes.

Endoscopes can also be used to carry out operations. To do this, tiny surgical instruments such as scalpels or forceps are inserted through another tube into another small incision. The surgeon uses the endoscope to watch what he or she is doing at the surgical site.

There are several advantages to doing endoscopic operations. Instead of the large incision needed in a regular operation, only a few small incisions, each less than a couple of centimeters long, are needed to insert the endoscope probe and other instruments. This means that there is less likelihood of nerve damage, as well as less bleeding and swelling. Patients also recover more quickly. An endoscopic breast reconstruction, for instance, can be carried out with just three or four short incisions (see pages 22–3).

> "You are looking at a flat TV monitor and operating a very thin instrument through very small holes in the tummy. So even just appreciating that and working in a three-dimensional space is very difficult."
>
> Abdominal surgeon Dr. Nick Taffinder

## Microsurgery

Microsurgery has allowed plastic surgeons to carry out incredibly delicate operations in which tiny blood vessels and nerves are rejoined. Before microsurgery, if you had a severed finger or a big open wound on your body, there was little that could be done. Today it is likely that the surgeon can rejoin the finger or take tissues from other parts of the body to repair the open wound.

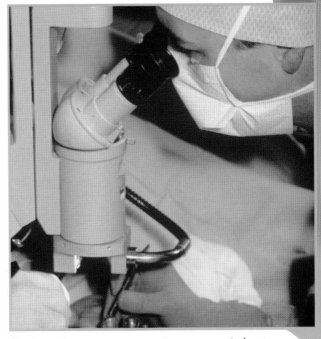

During microsurgery, operations are carried out while looking into a microscope. The needles and sutures used to stitch up wounds have to be small so that they do not damage blood vessels and nerves.

## Tissue flaps

One common procedure in reconstructive surgery is the removal of a piece of skin, muscle, and blood vessels from one part of the body for use in rebuilding another part. Such pieces of tissue are called flaps.

Tissues receive blood through tiny blood vessels called capillaries. The blood brings oxygen and nutrients to the tissue cells. When tissues are moved, the surgeon has to make sure that the cells have a blood supply; otherwise they will starve of oxygen and die. A tissue flap often also contains nerves, and these have to be reconnected so that the patient has feeling in the part of the body being rebuilt.

Sometimes a surgeon removes the blood vessels along with the tissues and then reconnects them when the tissue has been moved. The surgeon may even include large blood vessels in the tissue flap. Alternatively a tissue flap can be removed without a blood supply and then connected to local blood vessels in its new position.

Under normal conditions, a blood vessel that is cut or damaged will constrict (close up) to cut off the flow of blood. But blood vessels in a tissue flap have to be kept open at all times so that they can be connected in their new location. Surgeons keep the blood vessels open during tissue transplants by using a drug that stops the normal constriction response.

> *"When I first started there were no sutures, no needles, and no instruments small enough for surgery of this type. I used to make the needles myself under the microscope, and we borrowed or copied jewelers' instruments. A big breakthrough came from Silicon Valley and its microassembly techniques. Engineers were able to make needles for me that were thinner than a hair and drill the needle eye with a laser."*
>
> Dr. Harry Bunke, pioneer in the field of microsurgery

## Lasers

The laser is another important piece of equipment for the plastic surgeon. A laser produces a very intense beam of light of one wavelength (light of one color of the spectrum). A beam of laser light concentrates a large quantity of energy into a small space, making the laser a very powerful instrument.

Lasers are widely used in plastic surgery. The laser cuts through the skin like an ultra-fine scalpel. Its heat seals the blood vessels the instant that they are cut so there is little bleeding. The finely focused beam of light allows the surgeon to make very precise cuts.

A new trend in laser surgery is to use the special properties of different wavelengths of laser light to treat a range of problems. For example, red birthmarks known as port-wine stains can be treated using yellow laser light, which is more strongly absorbed by the red port wine stain than by other tissues. This means the birthmark can be destroyed without affecting the skin cells around it.

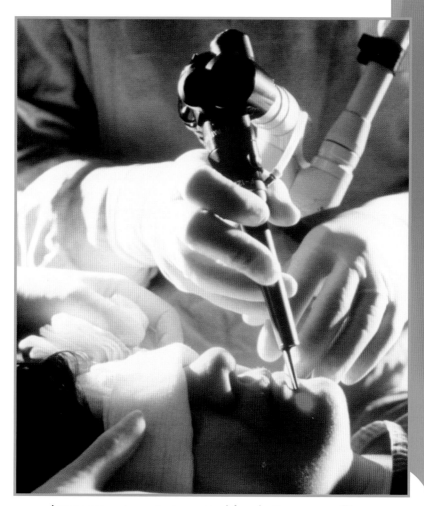

Lasers are an important new tool for plastic surgeons. They can be aimed at blood vessels or sent through optical fibers in endoscopes to reach areas that are very hard to reach. Here the laser is removing a mark on the skin.

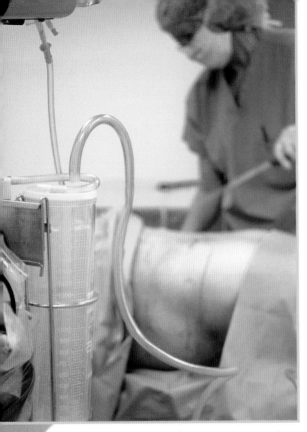

## Liposuction

One popular cosmetic procedure is liposuction, a technique for removing fat to reshape the body. Before liposuction was developed in the 1970s, fat deposits were removed by cutting them out with a scalpel, which often had uneven results and caused heavy bleeding. Today the surgeon injects the fatty area with a large quantity of anesthetic liquid that deadens the pain and causes the pockets of fat to become firm and swollen. A thin tube is then inserted into the area, and a vacuum pump sucks out unwanted fat.

Liposuction is the most common cosmetic surgery in the U.S. More than 478,000 procedures were performed in 2004. However, liposuction is not a substitute for diet and exercise, nor is it a cure for cellulite (the dimpled skin often found on the thighs, buttocks, and abdomen). Many consider it an unnecessary procedure.

Liposuction is a popular procedure used to remove fat from areas such as the stomach and thighs. As the name suggests, during liposuction, fat is sucked out of the body.

## Collagen implants

Collagen is a protein that helps give skin its elasticity and support. As skin ages, collagen is broken down or damaged, causing the skin to wrinkle. Doctors have found that it is safe to inject collagen and similar substances into the skin without the body rejecting them.

Collagen can be used to remove wrinkles as well as to enhance the lips. The collagen is injected into the edge of the lips, causing them to increase in size. Collagen can also be used to improve the appearance of hollow cheeks in patients suffering the side effects of various drug treatments. The effects of collagen injections are only temporary, lasting about three to six months. The implanted collagen is gradually broken down and reabsorbed by the body.

There are a number of synthetic materials that can be used in the same way as collagen. However, some people are allergic to these synthetic alternatives.

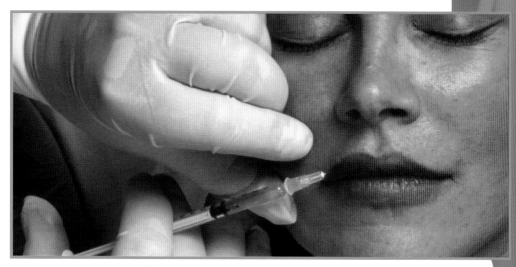

Collagen treatment involves injecting collagen into the skin using a very fine needle. The collagen fills out the skin and reduces the appearance of lines and wrinkles. Here the collagen is being injected to enhance the lips.

# Fighting rejection

Although collagen can be injected into the body without ill effects, in other areas of plastic surgery, rejection can be a major problem. Skin grafts are often rejected by the body. Initially, the grafted skin may look healthy and develop blood vessels, but sometimes the blood vessels break down, and white blood cells gather around the skin graft. (White blood cells help defend the body against disease.) A few days later the skin graft may begin to die. It is killed by the white blood cells and other body defenses, which do not recognize the graft as being part of the body.

Rejection of a graft can be prevented by using immunosuppressing drugs (drugs that stop the body's defenses from attacking the graft). However, such drugs leave the patient vulnerable to infection because they affect the whole body's immune (defense) system, not just the part rejecting the graft.

# Body Reconstruction

A few decades ago, a person badly disfigured in a fire or an accident would have had to live with the change in her or his appearance and the problems associated with it. Today, advances in reconstructive surgery mean that a surgeon can often rebuild the person's body and improve her or his quality of life.

## Injury, disease, and defects

A surprising number of people may need treatment during their lifetime for injuries to their face or body. For example, each year in the United States, millions of people suffer facial injuries. The majority of serious facial injuries affect young people and are caused by accidents, fights, or reckless behavior.

People also may require reconstructive surgery after treatment for cancer. Each year, thousands of women have to have cancer tissue removed from their breasts, but surgeons can now use various techniques to reconstruct the breast afterward (see pages 22–3). Mouth cancer affects the tongue, cheeks, and parts of the throat, and it also can cause disfigurement. Every year in the U.S., about 30,000 people are diagnosed with this form of cancer. Treatment can involve the removal of large areas of diseased facial tissue. The patients have to deal with both the disease and a disfigured face.

Thousands of babies are born each year with genetic defects such as a cleft lip and palate, double nose, or displaced eyes. These are called congenital (inherited) deformities. In countries with a good standard of medical care, these defects are routinely treated by reconstructive surgery.

> "It is thanks to micro-vascular surgery like this that we can now rebuild people's faces. Before, the bone grafts simply died. There has been a dramatic improvement in reconstruction over the past ten or fifteen years. We can now remove huge and aggressive cancers, and instead of leaving patients with a gaping hole in the side of their faces, we can rebuild them."
>
> Iain Hutchinson, maxillofacial surgeon

# Replantation

Replantation is the term used to describe the reattachment of a severed hand, foot, or even an entire limb. The operation to reattach the body part has to take place as quickly as possible after the accident that separated it. The severed part has to be kept clean and cold, although not freezing, as this delays the onset of permanent tissue damage. The surgical team is often large and usually involves plastic surgeons and orthopedic surgeons who deal with the bones and joints. First, the surgical team identifies all the tendons, bones, nerves, arteries, and veins, and cleans them so they are ready for repair. Any crushed tissue has to be removed, and broken bones have to be stabilized with metal plates. Using an operating microscope, the major arteries, veins, and major nerves are repaired and rejoined with sutures that are barely half the width of a human hair.

After the operation, the patient has to undergo physical therapy to restore muscle and nerve coordination. If the operation is successful, the patient will regain normal sensation, good muscular control, and strength. However, not all replantations are successful. The chance of success depends on the extent of the damage and the time since injury. Reattachment for a clean cut is more likely to be successful then reattachment for an injury in which a limb is crushed.

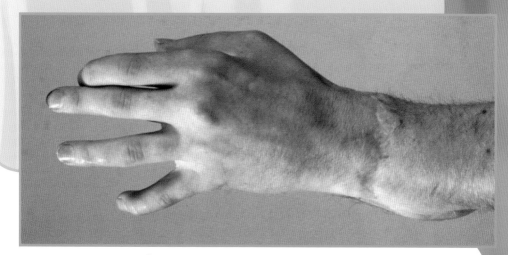

Surgeons trying to reattach a severed body part, such as a hand, have to restore blood flow to the part within about ten hours of the time of injury, otherwise the tissues will die. The operation itself lasts many hours.

## Cleft lip and palate

The word *cleft* means "split" or "separation." Congenital deformities such as a cleft lip and a cleft palate arise during the early stages of development of a fetus, when the two halves of the face develop separately and then join together. Sometimes the parts do not join properly, and this results in a cleft. A cleft lip is a split in the upper lip between the mouth and nose. The baby is operated on within the first few months of life. The skin and muscles of his or her lip are simply rearranged. A cleft palate occurs when the roof of the mouth has not joined completely. A cleft palate can make it hard for a baby to suck, so he or she feeds slowly and takes in too much air. In this repair the tissues are joined, and no extra tissue is required from other parts of the body. These patients may require further surgery on their jaws and nose as they grow up.

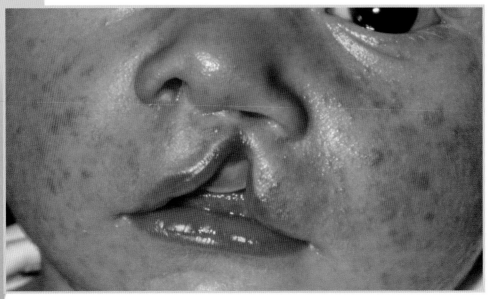

This baby has a cleft lip. The most common problem encountered during corrective surgery is when one side of the mouth and nose does not match the other side.

## Longer limbs

Occasionally, children may be born with deformities such as a short femur (thigh bone) or legs of unequal length. This causes back pain and hip problems as the body tries to make up for the loss. Russian surgeons have developed a new technique to replace missing bone and lengthen and straighten deformed bone. This technique can be used to

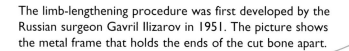

The limb-lengthening procedure was first developed by the Russian surgeon Gavril Ilizarov in 1951. The picture shows the metal frame that holds the ends of the cut bone apart.

increase the height of very short people by as much as twelve inches in the leg and five inches in the arm. The procedure involves cutting the leg or arm bones and gradually pulling them apart. The cut bones are then held apart using metal splints so that the ends do not move. The body repairs the break by laying down new bone tissue to fill the gap. In doing this, the length of the limb bones is increased.

Many people lose their fingers in accidents at work. Sometimes they can be sewn back on, but often people have to live without their fingers. The bone-lengthening technique has been adapted to stretch the stumps so that they regrow. The stump of the finger is broken and then pulled about a centimeter apart, leaving a gap in the bone. The finger is bolted in place with a metal frame, and the bone regrows to fill the gap. Unfortunately, it is impossible to restore a completely severed finger to its original length, as the skin would not be able to stretch enough, and joints would be needed to allow it to bend.

# Rebuilding the face

The aims of facial reconstruction are to repair bone, facial muscles, or skin; to restore functions such as swallowing or speech; and to restore the appearance of the face. In the early days of reconstructive surgery, metal was the material most comonly used. Modern techniques now allow specialist facial surgeons to remove tissues from other parts of the body and use them to replace missing tissue on the face. The jaw and cheekbones, for instance, may be rebuilt using bones from the ribs and shoulders.

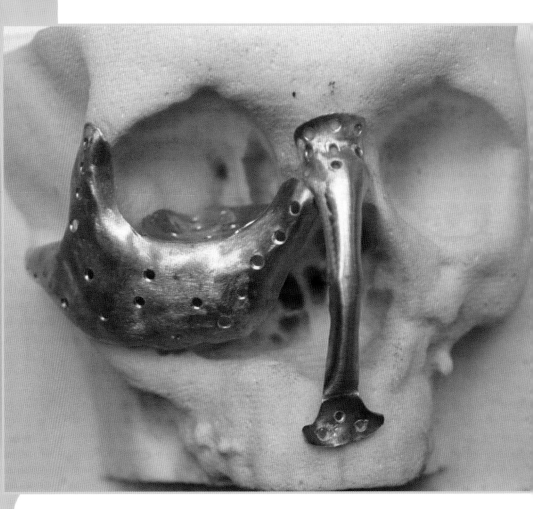

This picture shows the metal plates that were attached to the skull to form the cheek bone and nose during the rebuilding of a patient's face.

# Reusing bone and tissue

In one particular case, a patient named Constance had a fast-growing mouth cancer that had spread through her jaw. The surgeon removed half her jaw and her cheek to ensure that all traces of the cancer were removed. The reconstruction was carried out at the same time. A section of bone from the top of her left shoulder blade was shaped into a jaw and fixed in place with a large metal plate and metal screws. Surgeons were careful to leave the shoulder joint intact. A slice of skin from the back was removed to line the mouth. Microsurgery was used to join the tiny blood vessels attached to the grafted bone, each just two millimeters thick, to the carotid artery and jugular vein in the neck. Later Constance had false teeth implanted into her new jawbone and intensive speech therapy.

*"My husband and I were obviously very scared when we discovered I had cancer, especially when we were told that to cure it the surgery would mean removing virtually half of my face. I was told very delicately but left with no illusion how serious it was. It is amazing how my face has been rebuilt so well."*

Constance, recovering from mouth cancer

## Let's Face It

In 1977 Christine Piff was a busy mother with three young children. She developed a painful swelling in her left cheek, which was found to be a cancerous tumor. The cancer did not respond to radiation or chemotherapy, so she had to undergo surgery. This resulted in the loss of half her palate, her upper teeth, and her left eye. During this traumatic period, Christine felt that there was no one to talk to who had experienced something similar. She felt totally alone.

In 1984 Christine launched a new charity, Let's Face It, to provide support for children and adults who have a different face. Today the charity is international, with groups all over the world providing support. Its aim is to help people with facial disfigurements to share their experiences, to give them courage to cope with life, and to educate the public to value the person behind every face.

# Breast reconstruction

Approximately one in every eight women born in the U.S. today will develop breast cancer. The treatment of this cancer involves the removal of the diseased tissue from the breast. Depending on how far the cancer has spread, some women will need to have only part of a breast removed (a lumpectomy), but others may need to have the whole breast removed (a mastectomy).

Many women choose to have their breast reconstructed after such an operation. Studies have found that that the reconstruction helps women recover from the cancer by making them feel normal.

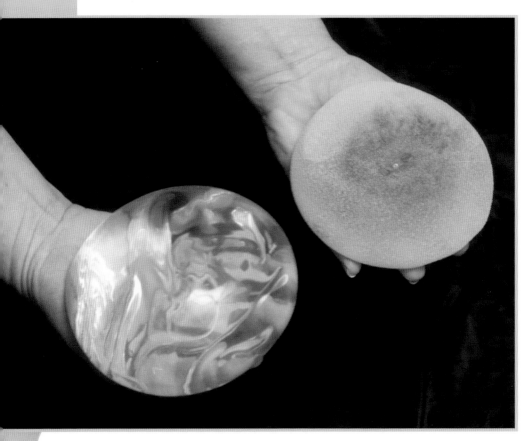

Breast implants come in various sizes and can be textured or smooth. The surgeon helps the patient choose the best one for her body type. The implant will be inserted under the skin.

# Methods of rebuilding the breast

There are three methods of breast reconstruction:

## Implants

Where enough breast tissue remains after surgery, it is possible to insert an implant under the skin. An implant is a plastic sac filled with sterile salt solution.

## Tissue expansion

Where there is little remaining breast tissue but the underlying muscles remain, a second method called tissue expansion can be used. This involves inserting an expandable implant under the chest muscle and gradually expanding it over a few months by injecting it with sterile salt water. This causes the skin and muscle to stretch. Once the desired expansion has been achieved, the expandable implant is replaced by a permanent implant.

## Flaps

The third method of reconstruction is used in cases where a woman has had all of the breast tissue and much of the underlying chest muscle removed. Areas of muscle and skin known as flaps are taken from the back or abdomen and used to rebuild the breast.

Breast reconstruction using flaps can be done in two ways. One way is to move the whole flap, with its blood supply still attached, by tunneling under the skin and onto the chest wall. The second method is called free flap reconstruction. In this method the flap is removed completely and the blood supply cut. This means that once the flap has been positioned on the chest wall, a new blood supply must be created, using blood vessels in the armpit or inside the chest. Very specialized microsurgery (see page 11) is needed to do this. The removal of flaps from the back or abdomen leaves large scars, and the shape of the body may be altered by the loss of tissue. However, these areas are usually covered by clothing.

# Coping with disfigurement

People cope with disfigurement in different ways. Some people feel that their lives will never be normal until their disfigurement is corrected. Others adapt to their disfigurement and come to believe that it is an essential part of their character, and that to alter it would change them. They do not want a surgeon to change their appearance.

There is no doubt that children can suffer many emotional difficulties from disfigurements, whether they are genetic or a result of injury. A child may suffer from low esteem or may be subject to teasing and bullying because he or she looks different. They may find it harder to make friends and be reluctant to speak in class or on the playground. Often children are regularly absent from school to attend medical appointments, and this disrupts their school life. However, many children are transformed after they receive corrective surgery.

One of the most common characteristics for which children are made fun of is their ears sticking out. Fortunately, in extreme cases, this can be changed through simple surgery, called ostoplasty, in which the ears are pinned back.

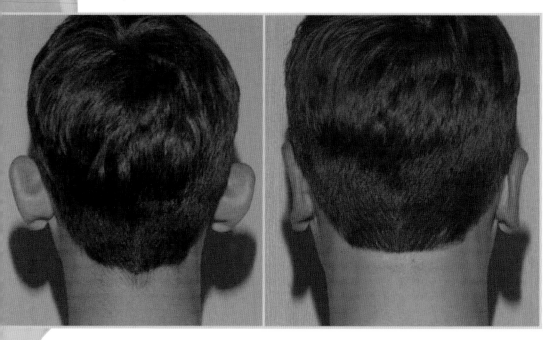

Here is a young boy before (left) and eighteen months after surgery to pin back his ears (right). In most cases, this procedure is simple and highly effective.

# Yes or no to reconstruction?

## Rhonda's story

Rhonda is one of the many patients who feel happier after their reconstruction. Rhonda's abnormality started as a teenager when the right side of her jaw grew much longer than the left side. Her face was completely lopsided, and her teeth did not meet. She was in continual pain and had difficulty eating. Her treatment started with wearing braces to move the teeth into the right place. A year later she had an operation to rebuild her face. Her upper and lower jaws were broken, and excess bone was removed from them. Then her nose was broken and rebuilt in the right place. A bone graft and six metal plates were used to fill out her cheek bones and to screw her jaw back together. The surgeon avoided scarring by working from the inside, making cuts in her mouth and peeling back the skin to expose the facial bones. The most difficult stage was probably Rhonda's appearance after the operation when her face was three times its usual size, with drains and tubes running from it. However, within six months her face had recovered.

*"I am really pleased with the outcome, and my friends all tell me I am much more confident now. It was certainly worth all the pain and discomfort, although I have to admit that I didn't think that immediately after the surgery."*

Rhonda, five months after her surgery

## Vicky's story

Vicky Lucas decided against reconstructive surgery. She has a rare disorder called cherubism, which affects the face. She found growing up with this disfigurement difficult, especially during puberty when her face became very large. So why has she turned down the opportunity to have a "normal" face? She says she would rather be extraordinary than simply ordinary and wants people to appreciate that her face is an important part of who she is. She has developed self-esteem and self-confidence and feels strongly that she shouldn't change her appearance just because of other people's attitudes toward her. Vicky has found that facial disfigurement is not just a medical issue, but a social issue as well. She realized that she was so unhappy, not because of the way her face looked, but because of the way some people would react to her face. She wants social attitudes toward disfigurement to change.

*"I am critical of a society that thinks the best thing to do—and the only thing to do—is for people with facial disfigurements to change themselves."*

Vicky Lucas

# New Skin

Healthy skin prevents the loss of fluid from the tissues beneath and is an effective barrier to infection. However, when the skin is burned, these functions are lost.

## Normal skin

The skin forms a protective covering over the body. It is made up of two layers, the epidermis and the dermis. The epidermis is the outermost part of the skin and is exposed to the environment.

Epidermal cells are made in the lowest layer of the epidermis. There, cells are continually growing and dividing. As new cells form, the older cells are pushed upward. As they move up, they die and then become filled with a substance called keratin. Keratin is a tough, waterproof substance also found in nails, horns, and hair. Therefore, the outmost layer of skin is made up of dead cells that are hard and waterproof. As these cells wear off, they are replaced by more cells from below. The tough top layer varies in thickness and is thickest on the soles of the feet.

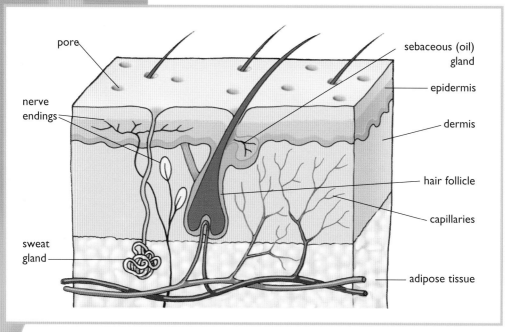

This diagram shows a cross-section of skin. A typical square centimeter of skin contains 15 hairs, 15 sebaceous glands, 100 sweat glands, 22 inches of nerves, and 500,000 dead and dying cells.

Some epidermal cells contain a dark brown pigment called melanin. Melanin protects the skin by absorbing harmful ultraviolet rays in sunlight. When the skin is exposed to ultraviolet light, the melanin spreads and the skin becomes darker and tanned. People who live in areas of the world where there is more sun have more melanin, which gives them dark skin.

The dermis is much thicker than the epidermis. It is made up of mostly connective tissue. Connective tissue, as its name suggests, joins all the structures found in the dermis, such as sweat glands, blood vessels, and nerve endings. It is criss-crossed by strands of collagen and another protein called elastin. Together they give the skin elasticity and firmness.

Beneath the dermis is a layer of fat-filled cells called adipose tissue. This helps keep the body warm by trapping heat. Adipose tissue also cushions the body from bumps and knocks.

Fat is also an energy reserve. If the body does not get enough energy from food, it breaks down the fat in adipose tissue to release energy.

# Types of burns

The seriousness of a burn depends on how deeply it has affected the tissue. There are three categories of burn; superficial, partial thickness, and full thickness (the most severe kind). These used to be called first-, second-, and third-degree burns. In the case of superficial and partial thickness burns, the skin can regenerate (repair itself). However, full-thickness burns damage the dermis, so regeneration is not possible.

After severe burns, fluid is lost through the skin as the tissues swell and the blood vessels become leaky. Blood volume and blood pressure drop, and this has a serious effect on the heart and circulation.

> *"Being burned is one of the most stressful things that can happen to the body. It causes a strong inflammatory response, like when you hit your thumb with a hammer and it gets all red and swollen . . . The amount of energy it takes to keep going is the same as that of a marathon runner. Imagine running a marathon 24 hours a day and never being able to stop."*
>
> Dr. David Heimbach, director of the burn unit at
> Harborview Medical Center, Seattle

# Skin grafts

Normally, people with full-thickness burns will need a skin graft. Skin grafts involve taking the full thickness of skin from healthy parts of the body and grafting that skin onto the burn wound. Sometimes a skin graft can be taken from the skin surrounding the injury, which is a better match for color and texture.

A graft is successful when new blood vessels and tissue form in the injured area. Unfortunately, skin grafts often fail. They may become infected and the tissues may die, or the whole skin graft may come away from the underlying skin as a result of pressure or movement.

Sometimes the damaged area lacks the blood supply needed for a successful skin graft. In these cases, a flap of skin together with underlying fat, blood vessels, and sometimes muscle is moved from a healthy part of the body to the burn site. When the flap is attached, the surgeons also reattach the blood vessels using microsurgery.

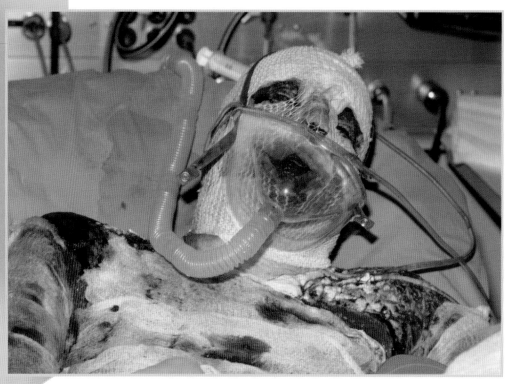

People with serious burns lose lots of liquid and often need intravenous fluids (fluids injected into their veins). They must be kept warm because a burned body cannot regulate (control) its temperature properly. They also must be protected from germs because burned skin cannot protect itself from infection.

## Some drawbacks

Skin grafts consisting of the epidermis and all the dermis (full-thickness grafts) can only be used for small areas. Also, the grafts can only be taken from parts of the body where scarring will not be visible, as the removal of the flap leaves a noticeable scar.

Large areas of damaged skin are treated using split-thickness grafts (the epidermis and only part of the dermis). Split-thickness grafts have several disadvantages. They tend to contract or shrink during healing, and they will not grow with the individual. The skin tends to be smoother and shinier than normal skin, and it may be an abnormal color—either very pale or white. If used to resurface large burns on the face, split-thickness grafts can produce an undesirable mask-like appearance. Finally, the wound created at the site from which the split-thickness graft is harvested is often more painful than the site to which the graft is applied.

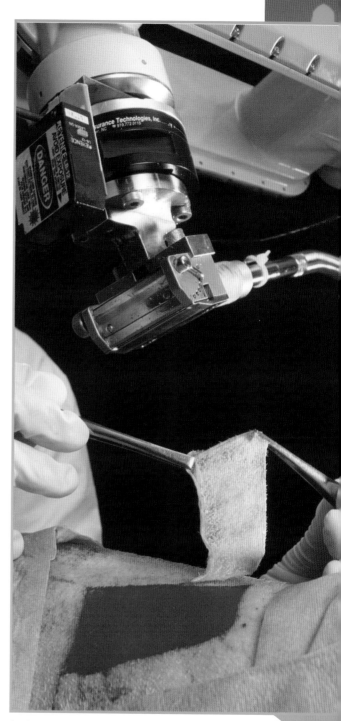

A skin-harvesting robot is being tested on the skin of a pig. The robot is removing a thin layer of skin for use in skin grafts. Harvesting skin is a tricky procedure, and using a robot should make it easier to produce skin grafts in the future.

29

## Artificial skin

If large areas of a person's skin are burned, there may not be enough healthy skin left from which to make grafts. In the past, skin taken from dead people was used to make grafts in such cases. However, there were problems, including rejection and infection. Nowadays, many burn patients are treated using artificial skin. One of the most useful artificial skins is one that can be used to treat full-thickness burns. This is a thin sheet containing collagen fibers and a substance that stimulates cell division and growth. The top layer of the artificial skin is silicone.

## Growing a new layer

First, the burned skin is removed to reveal healthy tissue, and then artificial skin is laid over the area, with the silicone layer on the outside. The artificial skin provides the framework for blood vessels and dermal skin cells to regrow into a new skin layer. Capillaries extend into the artificial skin, providing it with a new blood supply, while skin cells move in from the surrounding healthy areas, gradually forming new skin. The silicone layer temporarily closes the wound and protects against infection as well as controls water and heat loss.

Within three weeks, a new layer of dermal skin is produced and the silicone layer can be removed. Then ultra-thin pieces of epidermis are shaved off healthy areas of the person's skin and laid over the new dermal skin.

Unlike grafted skin, this new skin is flexible and will grow. The only limitation is that patients with large areas of new skin must avoid strenuous exercise in the sun, because the replacement dermis does not have sweat glands and hair follicles (roots). However, recent research has shown that hair follicles can be inserted into the new skin, so skin graft patients will be able to grow hair.

> "Burn patient survival rates have increased a lot over the last ten years. If you had that type of success rate with AIDS, there would be Nobel prizes all over the place."
>
> Scott Somers, head of the trauma and burn
> injury program for the National Institutes
> of Health's Institute of General Medical Sciences

# Culturing skin cells

Artificial skin cannot regenerate epidermis, only dermis. Therefore, it is still necessary to shave epidermal cells off the patient's own skin in order to complete the treatment. But now, epidermal cells can be grown in the laboratory and used to build an artificial epidermis.

First, a small area of skin is removed from a donor. The epidermal cells are separated and then grown in a special nutrient solution that causes them to multiply. Soon large numbers of epidermal cells, all identical to each other, have formed. Then they can be stored in liquid nitrogen. The cells are combined with collagen, which provides a framework for the epidermis.

Cultured epidermis can be grown to more than 100 times the area of the original sample, and it takes only 3 weeks to grow 3 square feet. This may then be grafted onto parts of the body where the epithelial cells have been destroyed. The cultured epidermis is applied over the patient's wounds and covered with a traditional burn dressing. The wounds heal within one to two weeks after grafting.

With this method it should soon be possible to grow cultured epidermis from the patient's own skin cells. This would lessen the chance of the patient rejecting the graft.

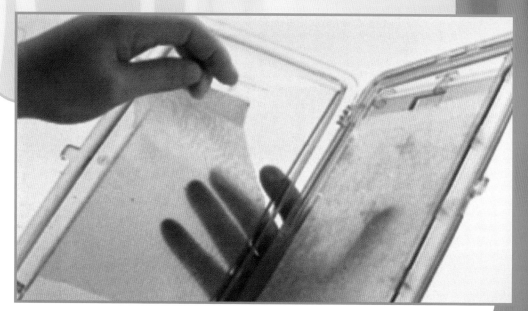

This artificial skin was made in a hospital laboratory in France. The thin layer of cultured epidermis is clipped to a piece of gauze to protect it until it is used.

# Cosmetic Facial Surgery

Your face is on display all the time, and it is usually the first thing people notice. Whether it is right or wrong, society prefers what it considers to be an attractive face. For instance, research has shown that attractive people are generally seen as being more intelligent and capable, so they often get better jobs. It is not surprising that people sometimes focus on the way they look, and that people who feel that their face is not attractive may want to change it.

The many ads for cosmetic surgery in magazines make it sound easy. Some procedures can even be carried out in a lunch hour! These ads make people think that they need surgery, even when they look fine. And surgery can be risky, especially when it is not necessary.

## Aging skin

Sometimes people have facial treatment to remove signs of aging. As you get older, your skin becomes drier and loses its elasticity. The underlying adipose tissue becomes thinner, so the skin begins to sag. It looks and feels less stretchy and becomes wrinkled.

So some people turn to one of a wide range of procedures that can reverse signs of aging. The face can be treated in various ways to remove the top layer of skin and reduce fine lines and wrinkles. However, the only permanent way to get rid of wrinkles is to have some form of surgery. This could be anything from removal of the bags under the eyes to a full facelift.

As people age, their skin starts to sag, and wrinkles form around their eyes and mouth.

## A fresh layer of skin

The least risky treatment for the face is a chemical peel. A chemical is applied to the skin, which causes the epidermal cells to blister and peel off over a period of fourteen days. The peeled layers are replaced by new skin, which is smoother and brighter.

Each year more than one million people in the U.S. have micro-dermabrasion. A spray of very fine dust, such as fine aluminum oxide, is applied to the skin. The dust and the dead skin are then vacuumed off. This treatment removes the top layer of skin along with spots, minor lines, large pores, and discolorations.

## Photorejuvenation

Light treatments, known as photorejuvenation, are used to treat skin with sun damage. This damage could be broken capillaries, which look like tiny spiders' webs on the surface of skin, or dark blotches and wrinkles. Photorejuvenation can also improve mild acne and reduce the size of large pores and fine lines.

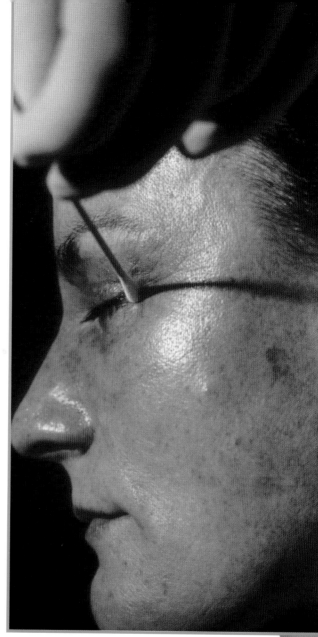

A chemical peel sometimes causes the skin to lose its ability to tan, and people given these treatments have to stay out of the sun.

The treatment consists of a series of intense pulses of light of a specific wavelength. The light is focused on the target area of skin—for example a broken capillary. The heat from the pulse destroys the target, leaving the surrounding tissue untouched.

# Botox

*Clostridium botulinum* is a bacterium that produces one of the most deadly human toxins (poisons) known. Its main effect is to paralyze the muscles. However, this deadly toxin has some important uses, both in cosmetic surgery and in the treatment of diseases affecting muscles.

Botulinum toxin is used to treat medical conditions caused by excessive, involuntary (not controlled by the mind) contraction of the muscles. It was originally approved to treat crossed eyes and uncontrollable blinking. Some people suffer from severe sweating of the palms of the hands and the soles of the feet, and botulinum toxin has proved to be an effective treatment because it paralyzes the sweat glands. Some celebrities have been known to have injections in their armpits to prevent their clothes from being stained by sweat patches!

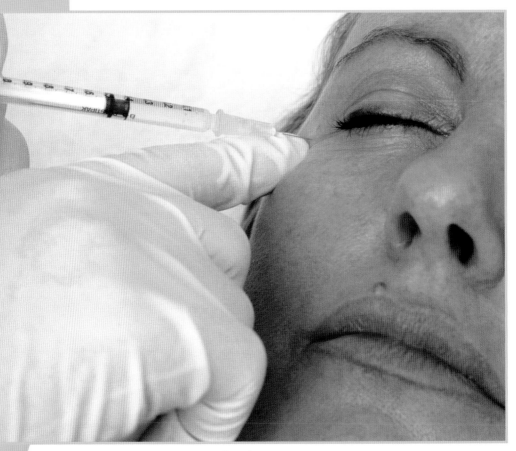

A fine needle is used to inject botulinum toxin into the creases around the eyes. As the muscles relax, the creases become less obvious.

Research is now looking at how botulinum toxin can be used to treat diseases of the nervous system—such as Parkinson's disease, Tourette's syndrome, and multiple sclerosis—where patients can suffer from uncontrollable movements.

# Weakening the muscles

However, the most common use of botulinum toxin is in cosmetic procedures to get rid of wrinkles and frown lines on the face. The treatment is commonly called Botox. A few drops of Botox® are injected into the muscle beneath a wrinkle. The toxin stops the muscle from working, so the muscle weakens and the skin over it relaxes. The result is that wrinkles soften and may disappear, but it also means that people who have had the treatment in their forehead, for instance, cannot frown. The toxin wears off after several months, but with repeated treatments the effects last longer.

Problems can occur with these injections. If they are given over a long period of time, they can cause facial muscles to weaken and lead to one side of the face drooping.

# Bags around the eyes

By far the most common plastic surgical procedure of the eyes is blepharoplasty. The procedure is relatively quick and has a high success rate. Blepharoplasty removes pouches of extra skin above and below the eyes, under a local anesthetic. For the upper lids, the surgeon makes an incision along the crease in the upper lid above the eyelashes, and then removes extra skin and fat. On the lower lid, the surgeon can either make an incision right under the eyelashes or inside the lid, which leaves no visible scar. Blepharoplasty is considered safe, but serious complications such as dry eyes, drooping eyelids, and even blindness occasionally occur.

# Rhinoplasty

Another popular facial procedure is rhinoplasty, which is commonly called a nose job. The surgeon makes an incision to gain access to the bone and cartilage of the nose. This can be on the underside of the nose (the part separating the nostrils) or on the inside. The bone and cartilage are then sculpted to the desired shape by removing, adding, or rearranging tissue. For example, the surgeon may fix a bump on the bridge of the nose by removing excess cartilage and trimming the bone. Rhinoplasty can also be carried out for medical reasons, to correct breathing difficulties, for example.

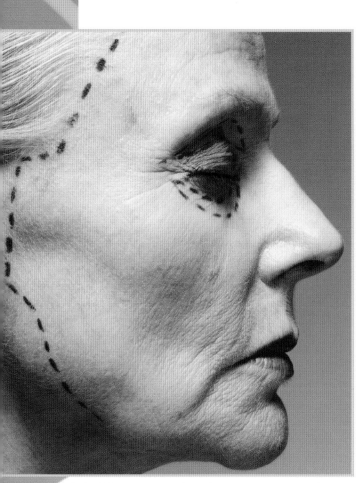

# Facelifts

As the face ages, the skin becomes less elastic, leading to wrinkles and sagging skin. Some older people have a facelift, or rhytidectomy, to try to reverse these signs of aging. With a successful facelift, the tightening of the skin and the underlying tissues can make a face look about ten years younger. But if it goes wrong, the face can look terrible.

Today's surgeons carry out facelifts using endoscopes. A number of small incisions are placed in areas where the most correction is needed. Usually this involves three or more puncture-type incisions at the hairline. Incisions can also be hidden in the lower eyelids, in the upper gum line, beneath the chin, and behind the ears. The endoscope allows the surgeon to release the muscles that produce frown lines and reposition the eyebrows at a higher level. Liposuction may be used to remove extra fatty tissue under the skin. Sometimes silicone implants may be positioned under the skin of the cheek or chin to improve the appearance of the face.

A facelift used to involve a long incision down the side of the forehead to the front of each ear and back into the hairline on the back of the head. This method often gave the patient a stretched look, with the skin around the eyes being pulled to the sides.

*"I'm not a facelift person. I just don't want to do it. For me the trade-off is that something of your soul in your face goes away. You end up looking body-snatched in the last analysis."*

Actor Robert Redford, 2002

# A face gone wrong

Surgical mistakes in facial procedures are usually very noticeable and often extremely difficult to repair. Mistakes can leave the patient looking wooden or unnatural. The surgery may cause scarring and misshapen facial features; for example, one eyebrow may be higher than the other, the skin may look too tight, or the whole face may end up asymmetric (uneven or lopsided).

Often surgical errors can be repaired, but there has to be enough tissue for this to take place, and the repair may be difficult. A poor nose job, for instance, can be impossible to fix. Patients may have to pay for the repair work, which might be more expensive than the original operation because the repair is technically more difficult. Even relatively simple procedures, such as collagen implants in the lips, can result in the lips looking unnaturally large. In some cases, patients experience an allergic reaction to the collagen, and their lips and lower face swell up.

Some people undergo a series of surgical procedures in order to achieve major changes to their appearance, but the results can sometimes look unnatural.

# The Perfect Body

In modern American culture, thin is considered beautiful. Magazines, television, and films all feature attractive young people with slim, toned bodies. For today's celebrities, having the right body is very important. Many feel that they will only succeed if they have a body that looks perfect on camera. They exercise and diet, and if that doesn't work, some resort to cosmetic surgery.

You have already seen that ideas of beauty differ among cultures, but the Western idea of beauty is spread around the world through television and film. The women of Fiji used to prefer rounded bodies, but in 1995 American television arrived in the islands. Within a short time many Fijian girls were describing themselves as too big or fat.

## Celebrity looks

For today's generation, the ideal body is probably one they have seen on television or in a celebrity magazine. It is not uncommon for young women to turn up at a consultation with a cosmetic surgeon complete with pictures torn from magazines. They ask the surgeon for breasts, lips, or curvy bodies like those of film stars and supermodels. It is also now more common for men to have similar expectations and want to have the looks and bodies of famous actors. These famous men and women often have features that, though they may be natural, look as though they have been surgically or computer-enhanced.

Sometimes the features of celebrities look great with makeup and reproduced in a photo or on television, but they can look unnatural in real life. With the advances in surgical techniques, it is becoming possible to create a body with the desired shape. For example, using the latest methods of liposuction, a surgeon can sculpt a person's body to look like someone else. However, there is the risk that the new shape could look odd on another person. More dangerously, surgery of any kind always carries serious risks to health.

# Designer exercise

The traditional ways of improving one's body shape or appearance are through diet and exercise. Dieting is one way to lose weight, while exercise helps with slimming and also toning the muscles. During exercise the body burns fuel, which it gets from fat reserves. With fewer fat reserves, the body becomes slimmer. Weight training can build muscle strength and mass, and this creates a greater change in body shape. Bodybuilders combine exercise with diet to increase their muscle bulk and remove fat deposits.

Increasing numbers of people in rich, developed countries are joining gyms to keep themselves fit. Hours of carefully designed exercise can lead to a muscular, sculpted body. However, many people have neither the time nor the drive to reach high levels of fitness. Instead they may turn to surgery to improve the way their body looks.

# Instant results

Exercise takes time and a lot of effort and willpower. Many people want an instant change rather than a gradual one, so they turn to cosmetic surgery for help. In other cases it does not matter how much a person exercises. Sometimes it is impossible to completely change a certain body feature. Some men, for instance, suffer from gynecomastia, an inherited condition that gives them enlarged, fatty breasts. Men with gynecomastia may also turn to surgery. Oversized breasts can also be a problem for women. The weight of the breasts can cause back, neck, and shoulder pain, and some large-breasted women are unable to participate in sports. The only way they can overcome this is to resort to surgery.

At the Seoul Olympics in 1988, Canadian sprinter Ben Johnson won the men's 100-meter final in 9.79 seconds. The time was a record that remained unbeaten until 2002. However, drug tests showed that Johnson had used steroids to achieve his record-breaking time. His gold medal was given to second-place Carl Lewis, and Johnson was banned from international athletics.

# Athletes and drug abuse

Drugs known as anabolic steroids (anabolic means building up) can speed up bodybuilding and enhance body shape. The hormone testosterone is a natural anabolic steroid, produced in a man's testes. One of its many roles is to increase muscle bulk. The first synthetic anabolic steroids were developed in the 1940s. They were first used to help the recovery of the many severely malnourished people released from prisoner-of-war and concentration camps at the end of World War II. In recent years a number of baseball players, bodybuilders, and other sports figures have abused these drugs, using them to artificially improve their performance.

## Anabolic steroids

Anabolic steroids work by increasing the amount of protein that the body produces, some of which goes into making more muscle. They also stimulate the production of red blood cells, and this increases the quantity of oxygen carried in the blood. Like most drugs, anabolic steroids have numerous side effects. For example they can cause acne, increased infertility in men, and increased masculinity and menstrual problems in women.

## Insulin

Recently, a number of athletes have started to use insulin as well as steroids. Insulin is one of two hormones that control the level of the sugar glucose in the blood. It is used medically to treat diabetes. Insulin causes glucose to be taken up from the blood into liver cells, where it is converted to a carbohydrate called glycogen. Glycogen is a quick-release energy store—it can be broken down during exercise to provide energy. In order to build up extra glycogen stores, some athletes and bodybuilders take glucose and insulin at the same time for a couple of hours shortly before a competition. However, the insulin can cause blood glucose to fall to dangerously low levels, causing the individual to collapse and go into a coma. This may lead to death.

Unfortunately, insulin is readily available and its use is not illegal, although it has been banned by the International Olympic Committee.

> *"Major League Baseball did nothing to take it out of the sport. Baseball owners and the players union . . . turned a blind eye to the clear evidence of steroid use in baseball."*
> Jose Canseco, ex-baseball player who admitted to using steroids, 2005

# Abdominal plastic surgery

Abdominal plastic surgery includes procedures to remove and tighten excess skin, fat, and muscle tissue. Some people choose to have abdominal plastic surgery in order to get rid of folds of loose skin that form after weight loss. Others have surgery because they have tried dieting and exercise but have stubborn areas of fat remaining.

Abdominal plastic surgery usually involves liposuction, or a tummy tuck (abdominoplasty), or both. A tummy tuck reduces the size of the stomach area. However, the incisions can be large, and the procedure can take time to heal. In some cases, abdominal plastic surgery is performed on a small area of the stomach, a procedure called a mini-tuck. This removes fat and tightens skin and muscles below the belly button.

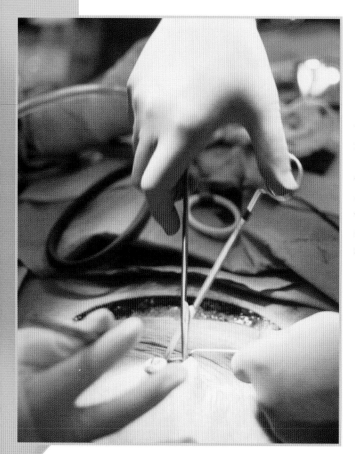

Some people choose a complete lower-body lift, which is a major procedure that leaves a large scar. The surgeon makes an incision around the entire abdominal area, so that excess skin can be removed and the hip, thigh, and buttock areas can be lifted. The result of the procedure is tightening of the back, hip, and abdominal tissues.

These surgeons are performing an abdominal mini-tuck. This kind of operation is less risky than a full tummy tuck because it involves only small incisions. A mini-tuck is usually combined with liposuction.

# Breast surgery

In recent years, breast enlargement has become one of the most frequently performed cosmetic procedures for women. Once again, the fact that a number of successful female celebrities have had breast enlargements has resulted in more women asking for the operation. In 2004 alone, more than 260,000 women in the United States had the operation. The current method involves the use of implants filled with saltwater. The surgeon makes an incision and slips a sterilized implant into a pocket under the breast.

A woman undergoing breast enlargement has to be aware of the risks. The incisions will leave scars, and there are sometimes side effects, such as swelling, bruising, bleeding, infection, and numbness or changes in feeling. She should also know that she may not be able to breastfeed after surgery, due to damage to the blood supply to the nipple.

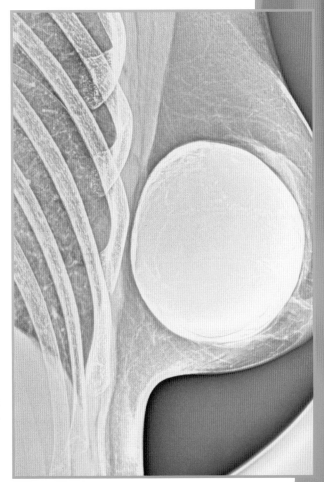

Men with gynecomastia (fatty breasts) may have an operation to reduce their breasts. In some cases the fat can be removed simply by liposuction, but usually there is some glandular tissue rather than just adipose tissue. In these cases, an operation is needed to remove the glandular tissue.

"If you have breast implants, you must expect to have another surgery in your lifetime. Deflation, infection— just about anything can happen."
Dr. Jean Loftus, a plastic surgeon from Cincinnati, Ohio

This X-ray of a woman's breast after enlargement surgery shows the implant.

# Problem implants

Silicones are polymers made from the element silicon. Silicone comes in a variety of forms, including gels (jelly-like materials) that were ideal for implants. During the 1980s thousands of women had silicone breast implants. Then in 1992, as a result of health scares, the U.S. Food and Drug Administration banned silicone breast implants. Silicone implants were replaced with implants containing saline (saltwater) solution.

There seemed to be a number of problems with silicone implants. The most serious were highlighted in a study that showed a link between silicone implants, breast cancer, and autoimmune diseases. Since that time, more research has been carried out, but experts still disagree over the safety of silicone implants. Silicone implants are used widely in Europe, but at the moment they remain illegal in the United States.

There are two other problems with implants. First, silicone implants do not last forever. Studies have found that as many as one in six implants burst after about five years and have to be removed. The second problem is called capsular contracture. This is the formation of excessive scar tissue around the implant, which leads to hardening and a change in shape of the breast. Further surgery has to be carried out to remove scar tissue and replace the implant.

# The J-Lo factor

Recently, the curvy backside of pop star and actress Jennifer Lopez caused a stir in the world of cosmetic surgery. Young women were demanding "a butt like J-Lo," and there was an increase in the number of women wanting buttock implants. The procedure involves the insertion of solid silicone implants between the main buttock muscles and their covering tissue. This creates a fuller and more rounded buttock. However, there are problems with these implants. Unlike a breast implant, the buttocks are subjected to more pressure, so there is a greater likelihood of the implant bursting. There may also be damage to the sciatic nerve running down the leg, which could lead to serious disability. Most patients have to wear a compression girdle (tight bandage) for several weeks while the tissues of the buttocks heal. Also, they cannot sit up properly for weeks until the swelling goes down.

"… The implants don't do well on an area we put so much pressure on like the buttocks."

Dr. Ed Luce, President of the American Society of Plastic Surgeons and Chief of Plastic Surgery at University Hospitals of Cleveland, Ohio

Although there has been a great deal written in the press about Jennifer Lopez's curvy backside, there has not been a general change in the Western idea that thin is beautiful.

# Cosmetic Concerns

Cosmetic surgery is a very competitive business, but for the patient it is full of pitfalls. Many people are won over by the glossy ads in magazines and newspapers, or the websites devoted to cosmetic surgery with their promises of improved looks. Often people agree to surgery without asking enough questions or checking out the surgeon's background or training.

## Cut-rate surgery

People may spend their life's savings on cosmetic surgery. A relatively simple Botox® injection can cost $400, and this has to be repeated every few months. A nose job can cost between $3,000 and $7,000, a breast enlargement up to $9,000, and a facelift can cost as much as $13,000.

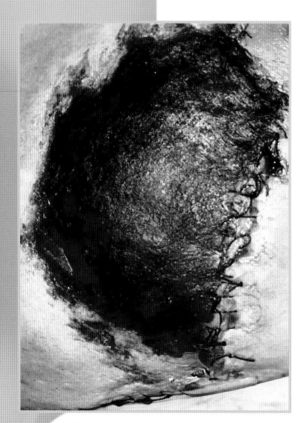

As costs rise, many people are tempted to go overseas, where clinics offer the same procedures for as little as a quarter of the usual price. Some people combine a vacation with surgery. A few people decide to go ahead with the procedures without checking the qualifications of the surgeon or the facilities offered by the clinic. Some of the procedures carried out are risky, and the clinic may not have the proper backup facilities if something goes wrong. In such clinics, post-operative care is often limited, and the patient may be sent home within a few hours.

One of the biggest risks in cosmetic surgery is infection. Some clinics have poor hygiene standards, and surgical equipment may spread infections. Poor-quality clinics can be less than helpful when things go wrong. Patients are often forced to go to their own doctor for treatment.

## New regulations

Because of the serious risks associated with bad cosmetic surgery, many people are pushing for new, nationwide regulations. But until the laws change, in most states any licensed doctor can perform plastic surgery, possibly even a dentist! So patients must make sure, on their own, that their plastic surgeon is certified by the American Board of Plastic Surgery. They also need to find out how long he or she has been performing the particular kind of surgery.

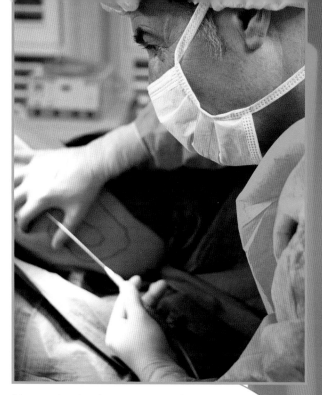

Liposuction has become a popular cosmetic procedure. The risks involved in this type of surgery have decreased but, as with all major surgery, an element of danger remains.

## The risks of liposuction

Risk is an important factor when considering cosmetic surgery. Most patients are perfectly healthy before surgery, so surgeons have to take all the possible risks into consideration when recommending surgery to a patient. For many years, liposuction was one of the more popular but risky cosmetic procedures. During the mid-1990s, one in every 139 liposuction patients experienced a complication such as a blood clot, fluid loss, infection, or a negative reaction to the anesthetic. There were even some deaths. The problem was linked to the sudden rise in the popularity of liposuction, which meant that many surgeons were carrying out the procedure without enough training or experience. However, the situation has improved, and the number of complications has declined. A recent study has found that fewer than one in 47,000 people undergoing liposuction died, and the complication rate has fallen to one in 384. But some people still might wonder if that is too large a risk to take.

## Unrealistic expectations

People decide that they want cosmetic surgery because they want to change part of their body. They expect the operation to improve their appearance. People may undergo surgery thinking that they are going to end up looking much younger or being several sizes smaller. If the surgeon does not give the patient a realistic idea of what can be achieved, the patient is bound to be disappointed by the surgery.

Cosmetic surgeons have to make difficult decisions when advising patients on surgical procedures. Surgeons are often visited by young women who are unhappy about the way they look and request operation after operation to improve an already attractive body.

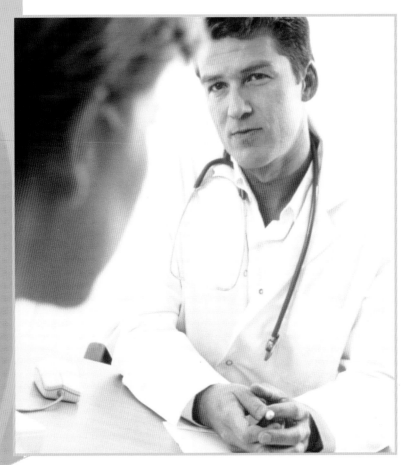

When deciding whether to have plastic surgery, patients cannot always rely on doctors' advice. Most cosmetic surgery is carried out privately, with the patient paying the doctor. Doctors stand to gain financially from the operation, so they may be tempted to encourage patients to have a procedure even though it may not be in the patients' best interest.

If they are turned away, they may visit others surgeons, or they may have surgery in a country where the regulations are less strict.

In many cases, there is nothing wrong with the person's appearance, and cosmetic surgery is rarely the answer. Some patients have a psychological problem that needs psychiatric treatment, not surgery.

In a few cases, people can have problems coming to terms with their much-improved appearance after plastic surgery, especially if they had been used to living with a badly disfigured face.

## Too young for surgery?

In 2001, a program on British television raised a storm of controversy when it reported that a teenager wanted to have her breasts enlarged when she turned sixteen, even though her breasts would not be fully developed by that age. The girl believed that she needed bigger breasts if she was to succeed later in life and that they would boost her self-confidence. Her parents supported her and agreed to pay for the surgery.

So was this girl unusual in wanting to improve her looks? Surgeons report seeing more teenagers who want to alter their appearance. Many people feel that procedures such as reshaping the nose or pinning back the ears may be okay for young people who feel they have awkward features and are suffering ridicule from their peers. But what about breast enlargement, eyelid surgery, or the removal of fat from the stomach and thighs?

Advertising and entertainment media can have a tremendous influence on people. Young people need careful guidance from parents and doctors when making decisions about plastic surgery. Sometimes parents can themselves be part of the problem. They want what is best for their child and often believe that cosmetic surgery is one way of improving the child's chances in life. One doctor reports that, on asking the question "Why don't you like your ears?", a child answered, "My father thinks they're too big." Surgeons have to deal carefully with cases such as this. They may insist on a waiting period to allow the young person to change his or her mind.

*"At the highest level of care, every surgery has risks as well as benefits"*

American Society of Plastic Surgeons

# Future Body

In the film *Face/Off,* the characters played by Nicholas Cage and John Travolta have their faces switched using laser technology. This may seem far-fetched, but it could be possible in the not-too-distant future. And face transplants are only the start. The body will always age, regardless of how much plastic surgery is carried out, so people may turn to more extreme ways of slowing down the aging process—perhaps even stepping into a new body! Such a development is perhaps far in the future, but other advances are being tested today.

## Growing fat

Why use a synthetic implant when fat can be taken from other parts of the body and used to enlarge the breasts or fill the cheeks? At the moment fat is not used for implants because it breaks down within the body. But in the near future, we may be able to remove adipose tissue from one part of the body, grow it to the right shape in the laboratory, then insert it into the breasts or buttocks.

Cultured adipose tissue could be used in facial reconstruction and face-lift surgery, too, to fill sunken cheeks, lines, and wrinkles. The collagen implants used today break down and have to be replaced, but adipose fillers would not have this problem.

In the film *Face/Off,* actors Nicholas Cage and John Travolta swap faces. The film is not real, but most of the technology to do such an operation is already available.

# Silkworms

Until adipose implants are available, surgeons will continue to use collagen, and a new source has been developed in Japan. Silkworms have been genetically modified so that instead of spinning cocoons made of pure silk, they produce cocoons that are ten percent collagen. The collagen is easy to extract, so this method could be used in the future to produce large amounts of collagen cheaply.

# Stem cells

Further in the future, advances in technology could allow plastic surgeons to produce cosmetic implants that would make adipose tissue implants seem primitive. Cells could be taken from the patient, grown in the laboratory, and then formed into implants for insertion back into the body.

The cells that are of greatest interest to scientists are stem cells, shown below, magnified 100 times. In humans, the cells of specialized tissues such as muscles and nerves become unable to divide once they are fully developed. But the cells are constantly dying and need to be replaced. New cells are supplied by stem cells, which continually divide to provide the replacements for cells that die.

Some stem cells have the ability to form other specialized cell types as they multiply. This means that a group of stem cells could be used to produce a number of different tissues. Some might be used to grow new bone, while others might form muscle. The stem cells would be grown on a framework to create an implant that would fit perfectly. The body would not reject the implant or form scar tissue around it because it would be made from the

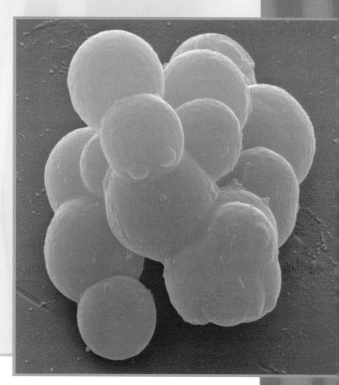

# Face transplants and beyond

According to some leading surgeons, full face transplants are no longer science fiction fantasy. They believe that such an operation would actually be possible. New drugs make it possible to stop the body's immune system from rejecting a transplanted face. Microsurgery could transplant new skin, bone, nose, chin, lips, and ears from dead donors to patients disfigured by accidents, burns, or cancer. One of the possible techniques would involve transplanting a kind of skin envelope of fat, skin, and blood vessels onto the existing bone, leaving the patient with many of her or his own features. A more complex procedure would be required to transplant the underlying bone as well, so that the patient would end up resembling the donor.

But would there be any donors? Many people when asked said that they could accept the procedure, but few would be willing to donate their face after dying. A large part of one's identity is connected to a person's face, so face transplants could also cause psychological problems for the patient receiving the face.

*"There are so many people without faces … but we are all so much more than just a face … you don't take on their personality. You are still you. If we can donate other organs of the body, then why not the face? I can't see anything wrong with it."*

Christine Piff, who founded the charity Let's Face It after suffering a rare facial cancer

# A whole new body?

Face transplants are just the start. Some doctors are thinking of more radical surgery that would involve transplanting the whole head, including the brain. Such a procedure could be used to treat people with diseases that affect the body but not the brain. Obviously this would be an incredibly complex process and is beyond current abilities. But with the advancement of microsurgery, it seems that nothing will be impossible in the future. The Open University's Millennium Project in Great Britain has worked with experts to forecast the changes we will see in the new millennium. It predicts that in the future organ-manufacturing skills could be used to build a new body for the brain.

In fact, the first brain transplant has been carried out. It was performed on a monkey. In 2001, professor Robert White from Cleveland, Ohio, transplanted a head containing the intact brain of a monkey onto another monkey's body, and the animal survived for some time after the operation. Professor White would like to be able to carry out a similar operation on humans, but many in the medical field consider the experiments dangerous and unnatural.

# Virtual reality

Computers already have an important role to play in plastic surgery, in particular the area of virtual reality. Virtual reality aims to show the user a computer-generated environment. The user wears a helmet linked to a computer with a head-mounted display showing the scene. The user may wear gloves or even a body suit that is also connected so that she or he can feel the environment as well as hear and see it.

Soon there will be virtual reality training programs for plastic surgeons. For example, surgeons in training will be able to practice medical procedures such as making incisions and connecting blood vessels using virtual reality, before operating on a live patient.

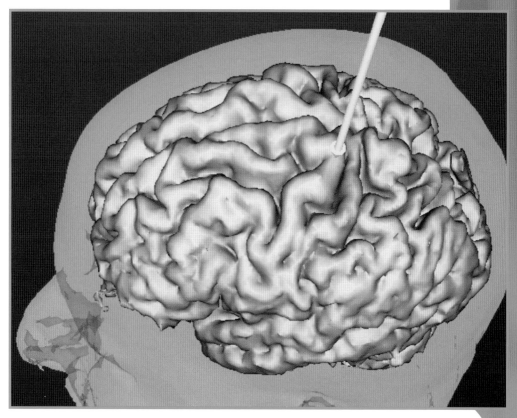

In virtual reality, three-dimensional images allow the surgeon to visualize an operation before carrying it out. By wearing virtual reality gloves, the surgeon can even get the feel of carrying out the actual procedure.

## Simulations

Increasingly, patients will use virtual reality to see exactly how their new cheeks, breasts, or lips will look. Once they have created their own 3-D character on screen, the medical team will use it to make implants. The surgery itself could be carried out by robots via remote control, allowing specialists to operate on patients hundreds of miles away—or even in another country! Robots are already being used in some kinds of surgery, so it will not be long before they are being used in plastic surgery.

## Virtual reality suits

A virtual reality suit has devices that create for the user the sights, sounds, and sensations of the artificial world and send information about what he or she is doing to the computer. Inside the helmet are tiny TV screens that allow users to see 360 degrees as they turn their heads. The sensory glove sends information about a user's hand movements to the computer, which then instructs the glove to create a sensation, such as tapping a finger on a hard surface.

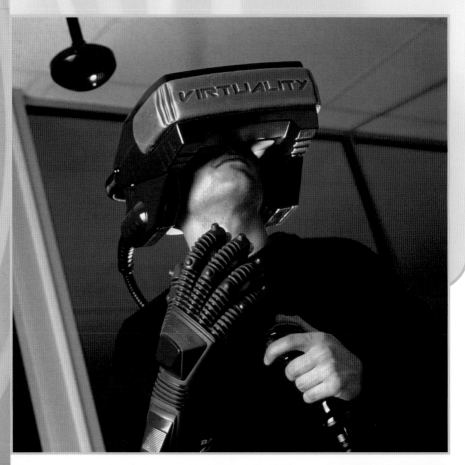

Virtual-reality simulations have already been used to reconstruct the face of a young boy whose features were destroyed by cancer. First the patient was placed in a magnetic resonance imaging (MRI) scanner to obtain detailed images of the tissues inside his head.
Then the imaging data was fed into the simulation, which allowed the surgeons to visualize how the soft tissues fitted over the bone and how the face would appear after surgery. By practicing the procedures beforehand using a simulation, the surgeons were much better able to carry out the actual surgery. In the future, with more computer power, surgeons will be able to work on larger areas of the body.

## Perfect children

As our ability to move and re-arrange genes improves, it is possible that within a few generations, parents may be able to design their own children. This would be the most extreme form of body sculpture—designing a new individual from scratch. However, this raises many issues. Should parents be able to remove certain genes from their embryos? Should they be allowed to go further and create a child with a particular appearance? Or should society prevent human control of genetic material and leave it to nature?

Perhaps the most worrying aspect of genetically engineering children is that it would probably reduce the genetic diversity of the human race—in other words, how different we are genetically from one another. It is likely that, given the choice, people would choose within a small number of highly valued characteristics for their children. In time, some genetic characteristics would be lost altogether. Also, a population of people who were genetically similar would be less able to deal with unexpected changes in their environment, such as the outbreak of a new disease.

> "As soon as the geneticists can change an embryo to produce a blond, blue-eyed, long-limbed baby, there will be a customer. But the future population of Barbie dolls won't be necessarily content. In my experience perfection often leads to more insecurity—and ultimately more surgery."
>
> Kathy Phillips, health and beauty director at *Vogue*

> "Design a body? It may be possible. I can do anything."
> Kevin Montgomery, computer engineer at the National Biocomputation Center of Stanford University, California

# Final Thoughts

Sue Morgan Elphick suffered from a facial deformity that made her lower jaw stick out beneath her upper. At the age of 30, she was a nurse at St. Bartholemew's Hospital in London, working for a plastic surgeon who specialized in reconstructing faces. One day the surgeon suggested he should reconstruct her face. To do this, he had to break nearly every bone in her face, and then fasten them together again with strips of titanium.

The reconstruction was incredibly painful, but a great success. Before her surgery, many people assumed Sue was unhappy, although in fact she was funny and outgoing. Today most people see Sue as an energetic, attractive woman. This shows how much we form our opinions of a person's character on the basis of his or her looks.

## A cosmetic future?

Advances in reconstructive surgery have filtered through into cosmetic surgery, leading to huge increases in the demand for cosmetic surgery during the last ten years. Businesses that specialize in plastic surgery take in a lot of money, and clinics are springing up around the world. By far the greatest number of these are in the United States and Europe, but more clinics are being set up in Eastern European countries, Australia, South Africa, Mexico, South America, and Asia. Cosmetic surgery is popular in China in particular. In 2004, the country held its first annual Artificial Beauty Pageant. Only women who have had extensive cosmetic surgery may enter.

A worrying trend is that the age of the patients having cosmetic surgery is decreasing. In the past, the majority of patients were older people wanting to look younger. Now, increasing numbers of younger people are choosing plastic surgery in order to improve their appearance. It is becoming more acceptable to have cosmetic surgery. But is this a good thing?

The huge market for cosmetic surgery is a result of society's obsession with image. Every day you are faced with hundreds of pictures of seemingly flawless faces and

Contestants line up for a chance to be crowned Miss Artificial Beauty in China, 2004. As cosmetic surgery becomes more popular, will pageants like this become more common? Some people worry that the pressure to look perfect will only lead to more dissatisfaction.

bodies. In the future, this obsession with perfect looks could lead to genetic engineering and so-called designer babies.

## Accepting differences

In this society, people with disfigurements are often seen as abnormal and suffer from other people's attitudes toward them. For many people with a disfigured face or body, it is the way other people react to them that bothers them most, not their actual disfigurement. Plastic surgery often helps people with disfigurements, but perhaps a better approach would be to educate people to accept physical differences and look beyond the surface to the personality beneath. If society valued people less for their appearance and more for who they are, perhaps fewer people would feel the need for cosmetic surgery in the first place.

# Timeline

| | |
|---|---|
| 1827 | Dr. John Peter Mettauer performs the first cleft palate operation in North America with instruments he designed himself. |
| 1838 | The term *plastic surgery* is first used in the surgical manual *Handbuch der Plastischen Chirurgie*, published by Zeiss. |
| 1881 | Edward Talbott Ely performs the first correction of sticking-out ears on a twelve-year-old boy at the Manhattan Eye, Ear, and Throat Hospital in New York. |
| 1896 | Jacques Joseph (born Jakob Lewin Joseph) reduces and pins back the ears of a boy with large ears that stick out. Two years later he carries out a nose reduction on another patient. He becomes known as the father of modern facial plastic surgery and a leading facial surgeon in Europe. |
| 1914–18 | During World War I, French army surgeon Hippolyte Morestin establishes a treatment center for wounded soldiers in France. A similar unit is set up at Aldershot Military Army Hospital in Hampshire by Sir Harold Gillies and Sir William Arbuthnot Lane. This becomes the first center of facial plastic surgery. |
| 1940 | The botulinum toxin is isolated. |
| 1949 | First breast implant using a polyvinyl alcohol sponge is carried out. |
| 1961 | The use of **silicone** implants is reported by Thomas Cronin. |
| 1962 | Ronald A. Malt performs the first successful replantation of an entire limb, on a twelve-year-old boy whose arm had been severed in an accident. |
| 1964 | Dr. Harry Buncke reports the first successful rabbit-ear replantation to the Plastic Surgery Research Council Meeting in Kansas City, Kansas. This was the first successful reattachment of an amputated part involving blood vessels less than one millimeter in diameter. |
| 1969 | Dr. Harry Buncke and Donald McLean perform the first successful microvascular tissue transplant during the repair of a defect of the scalp. |

| 1970 | Professor Earl Owen carries out the first re-attachment of an amputated finger. |
|---|---|
| 1972 | Two Japanese surgeons, Harii and Ohmori, carry out the first successful free skin flap transplant in a human. |
| 1974 | Dr. Giorgio Fischer carries out liposuction. |
| 1976 | Injectable collagen is used for the first time. |
| 1986 | Dr. David Heimbach at Harborview Medical Center in Seattle leads the team carrying out the world's first clinical trial of a new artificial skin, later called Integra. |
| 1987 | Jeffrey Klein introduces a new method of liposuction that involves the injection of an anesthetic liquid. This allows for more fat to be removed, while reducing blood loss. |
| 1989 | Botulinum toxin is approved by the Food and Drug Administration (FDA) for the treatment of crossed eyes in adults and certain facial spasms. |
| 1992 | The FDA declares a ban on silicone implants. |
| | Monte Keen, the director of facial, plastic, and reconstructive surgery at the Columbia Presbyterian Medical Center in New York is the first doctor to use botulinum toxin as an anti-wrinkle treatment. |
| 1998 | Dow Corning, one of the largest manufacturers of silicone breast implants, settles a class action lawsuit for $3.2 billion for 170,000 women who suffered serious side effects after surgery. |
| 1999 | The U.S. Institute of Medicine issues a 400-page report that concludes that silicone breast implants do not cause major illnesses. They are no longer used in the U.S., however, due to their tendency for silicone implants to leak or rupture, which leads to infections, hardening, and breast tissue scarring. |
| 2001 | Professor Robert White of Cleveland, Ohio, transplants the head containing the brain of a monkey into another monkey's body, and the animal survives for a few days. |
| 2002 | Silkworms are given the gene to produce collagen. The modified silkworms produce cocoons that are ten percent collagen. |
| 2005 | Surgeons in Cleveland, Ohio, begin preparing to do the first face transplant on a patient, using a face from a dead donor. |

# Glossary

**adipose tissue**  tissue made up of cells containing fat

**anesthesia**  drug that causes the loss of sensation in part of the body or all of the body before surgery

**autoimmune disease**  disease in which the body produces antibodies that act against its own cells; for example, rheumatoid arthritis and Acquired Immune Deficiency Syndrome (AIDS)

**blepharoplasty**  (pronounced *blef-ar-o-plas-tee*) cosmetic procedure to remove baggy skin around the eyes

**cancer**  disease in which the abnormal and uncontrollable growth of cells forms a tumor or growth

**carbohydrate**  molecule that contains carbon, hydrogen, and oxygen. Carbohydrates are used by the body as a source of energy.

**cell**  smallest functional unit of the body, consisting of a nucleus and cytoplasm bound by a membrane

**cellulite**  lumpy or dimpled fatty tissue, often found on the upper thighs, hips, and buttocks

**collagen**  type of protein that helps maintain skin's structure

**cultured**  grown in the laboratory

**dermis**  lower layer of the skin that contains the sweat glands and capillaries

**diabetes**  medical condition in which the pancreas fails to produce insulin, causing the blood glucose levels to rise

**elastin**  type of protein with elastic (stretchy) properties

**endoscope**  surgical instrument for viewing inside the body

**epidermis**  outermost layer of the skin with cells that contain the pigment melanin

**facelift**  cosmetic surgery in which the skin is tightened to remove wrinkles from around the eyes, nose, and mouth

**fetus** stage before birth in the development of a mammal. In the case of a human baby, the embryo becomes a fetus at eight weeks.

**flap** section of skin with muscle, blood vessels, and nerves attached that is taken from a healthy part of the body and used to rebuild a damaged part

**genetic** inherited, passed down from the mother and father in genes

**genetic engineering** process by which the DNA (genetic makeup) of an organism is altered by scientists. This can be achieved by inserting a gene taken from another organism or by removing a gene.

**genetically modified** DNA that has been altered artificially in the laboratory

**graft** transplant living tissue onto a damaged area of the body; for example, a skin graft in which healthy skin tissue, taken either from the same person or a donor, is laid over damaged skin

**hormone** chemical message produced by cells and transported in the blood to target cells where the message brings about an effect

**Human Immunodeficiency Virus (HIV)** the virus that causes Acquired Immune Deficiency Syndrome (AIDS) in humans

**insulin** hormone that controls the levels of glucose in the blood. A lack of insulin causes diabetes.

**laser** instrument that creates an intense beam of light of a specific wavelength; used in surgery to cut open tissue or remove blemishes

**liposuction** the removal of fat from the body using a suction technique

**magnetic resonance imaging (MRI) scanner** machine that uses a strong magnetic field to generate images of the inside of the body

**microsurgery** delicate surgery carried out on tissues, blood vessels, and nerves using a microscope and very small instruments

**optical fibers** thin glass fibers through which light can be transmitted

**paralyze/paralysis** condition in which impulses do not travel along nerves, preventing muscles from working

**polymer** compound made of one or more large molecules that is formed from repeated units of smaller molecules

**protein** large organic molecule made up of chains of amino acids

**puberty** period in development when a girl's or boy's body begins to change and become more like an adult's

**rejection** when the body's defense (immune) system reacts against a transplanted tissue or organ so that it does not survive

**rhinoplasty** procedure to reshape the nose

**rhytidectomy** complete facelift

**scalpel** sharp blade used by surgeons

**selective breeding** careful selection of individuals with certain characteristics to be the parents of the next generation. In time, the appearance of the species or variety changes to take on those selected characteristics.

**Silicon Valley** area in California where a large number of high-tech (computer) industries are located

**silicone** substance produced when silicon is combined with oxygen, carbon, and hydrogen

**stem cell** cell that has the ability to grow into a number of different types of specialist cells

**suture** stitch used to close a wound

**synthetic** artificial, made by a chemical process

**testes** parts of the male sex organ where sperm is produced

**testosterone** steroid hormone, produced in the testes, which is involved in the production of sperm and is responsible for male sexual characteristics

**tissue** group of cells of the same type that act together to carry out a particular role; for example, liver tissue and epidermal tissue

**transplant** when living tissues or organs are removed from one part of the body, or from another body, and surgically attached

**virtual reality** software that makes something appear to exist when it really does not

**wavelength** distance between two peaks or troughs of a wave. The shorter the distance, the shorter the wavelength.

# Further Reading

## Books

Fullick, Ann. *Science at the Edge: Frontiers of Surgery.* Chicago: Heinemann Library, 2005.

Morgan, Sally. *Science at the Edge: Cloning.* Chicago: Heinemann Library, 2002.

Many magazines such as *New Scientist, Odyssey,* and *Science* write informative articles about plastic surgery.

## Websites

A number of websites have up-to-date information on plastic surgery:

**http://www.surgery.org/index.asp**
The American Society for Aesthetic Plastic Surgery (ASAPS) is the leading organization of plastic surgeons specializing in cosmetic plastic surgery. The website provides unbiased information on many different cosmetic techniques.

**http://www.aafprs.org**

The American Academy of Facial Plastic and Reconstructive Surgery (AAFPRS) is the world's largest association of facial plastic and reconstructive surgeons.

**www.savingfaces.co.uk**
The Facial Surgery Research Foundation is a charity that researches into the prevention and treatment of oral and facial diseases and injuries.

# Index